I Pick Fall Pumpkins

by Mary Lindeen

first step nonfiction

Lerner Publications ◆ Minneapolis

LERNER

SOURCE™

Expand learning beyond the printed book. Download free, complementary educational resources for this book from our website, www.lernerresource.com.

The images in this book are used with the permission of: © iStockphoto.com/Kativ, p. 4; © iStockphoto.com/jamesvancouver, p. 5; © Marilyn Volan/Shutterstock.com, p. 6; © elegeyda/ Shutterstock.com, p. 7; © Jason O. Watson/Alamy, p. 8; © Malgorzata Litkowska/Shutterstock. com, p. 9; © ASAblanca/Getty Images, p. 10; Ingram Publishing/Newscom, p. 11; © Digital Vision/ Thinkstock, pp. 12, 14; © Jupiterimages/Getty Images, p. 13; © iStockphoto.com/Linda Kloosterhof, p. 15; © mikledray/Shutterstock.com, p. 16; © KellyNelson/Shutterstock.com, p. 17; © Denise Torres/ Shutterstock.com, pp. 18, 21; © iStockphoto.com/Terry Wilson, p. 19; © Ryan McVay/Getty Images, p. 20; © iStockphoto.com/Photographer, p. 22.
Front cover: © iStockphoto.com/Docbombay.

Main body text set in ITC Avant Garde Gothic Std Medium 21/25.
Typeface provided by International Typeface Corp.

Lerner Publications Company
A division of Lerner Publishing Group, Inc.
241 First Avenue North
Minneapolis, MN 55401 USA

For reading levels and more information, look up this title at www.lernerbooks.com.

Library of Congress Cataloging-in-Publication Data

Names: Lindeen, Mary, author.
Title: I pick fall pumpkins / by Mary Lindeen.
Description: Minneapolis : Lerner Publications, [2016] | Series: First step nonfiction. Observing fall |
    Audience: Ages 5–8. | Audience: K to grade 3. | Includes index.
Identifiers: LCCN 2015036034| ISBN 9781512407969 (lb : alk. paper) | ISBN 9781512412147
    (pb : alk. paper) | ISBN 9781512409956 (eb pdf)
Subjects: LCSH: Pumpkin—Juvenile literature.
Classification: LCC SB347 .L56 2016 | DDC 635/.62—dc22
LC record available at http://lccn.loc.gov/2015036034

Manufactured in the United States of America
1 – CG – 7/15/16

Table of Contents

Picking Pumpkins

It is fun to pick pumpkins
in the fall.

A field where pumpkins grow is called a pumpkin patch.

Pumpkins grow on a **vine**.

They are **ripe** and ready
to pick in the fall.

Pumpkins can be orange.

Pumpkins can be red.

Pumpkins can be white.

Pumpkins can be black.

Pumpkins can be blue too!

Some pumpkins are small.

Some pumpkins are tiny.

Some pumpkins are big.

All pumpkins need soil, sunshine, and water to grow.

Some pumpkins are huge!

Parts of a Pumpkin

A pumpkin has a **stem** at one end. The stem connects to the vine.

16

The outside of a pumpkin is called the **skin**. It is hard and bumpy.

17

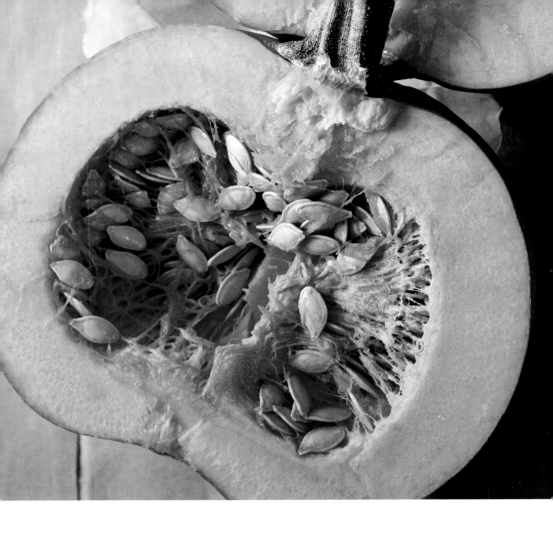

The inside of a pumpkin is soft and mushy. It is called
the **pulp**.

These seeds can be planted to grow new pumpkins next year.

Lots of seeds are also inside a pumpkin.

Eating Pumpkins

Some pumpkins are for eating. This pumpkin pie is soft and sweet.

Pumpkin seeds
are good for you!

These pumpkin seeds are
salty and crunchy.

What do you like best about pumpkins?

Glossary

pulp – the soft, juicy part of a fruit or vegetable

ripe – ready to be harvested, picked, or eaten

skin – the outer covering of a fruit or vegetable

stem – a part of a plant that supports the fruit

vine – a long, winding plant that grows along the ground or climbs on a fence, tree, or other support

Index